PURIFYING CRYSTALS

*How to clear,
charge and purify
your healing crystals*

Michael Gienger

EARTHDANCER

A FINDHORN PRESS IMPRINT

Contents

The Skilled Use and Handling of Healing Crystals

It was a phenomenon nobody had anticipated; I had passed on to a friend a Heliotrope crystal (bloodstone) that had been of good service to me on several occasions for treating colds. I cannot remember the exact reason why I gave it to him, but I distinctly remember the effect! No sooner had my friend hung the crystal on a leather thong around his neck, when he began to experience symptoms of a cold. This happened so quickly that luckily he was struck with the idea of removing the crystal. Lo and behold, the cold symptoms disappeared as fast as they had appeared. He applied the crystal again – the symptoms came back; he took the stone away – the symptoms went away. This he repeated several times. Naturally, in the end, he laid the crystal aside and made the inevitable phone call to me saying, 'For goodness sake, what kind of crystal have you given me?!'

I didn't know. What was the matter with the crystal? According to everything I knew, Heliotrope was a crystal that was supposed to help with colds, so why was it triggering these symptoms? Was this something like we see in homoeopathy, where you trigger in a well person those symptoms of illness that will heal someone who is ill? We immediately tried out a different Heliotrope crystal and the effect did not occur. We went back to the first specimen – promptly the cold symptoms returned. Something appeared to be *attached* to that crystal, and only that crystal, which was not the case with other Heliotrope crystal specimens. I thought about the colds I had actually cured with that precise crystal, but it brought us no closer to understanding. Possibly the crystal had stored 'information about the illness'. But how? And more importantly, how were we to get rid of that information?

I began to research this phenomenon and was greatly surprised by how many sources I found on the subject of storing and eliminating information in sensitive substances. Apparently this subject has been known about since ancient times, and there have always been the same hints and pointers on how to get rid of undesirable 'information'. Cleansing with incense seemed by far the most favoured method all over the world, followed by cleansing with salt, which took up ten pages alone in a handbook on German superstitions that was a veritable encyclopaedia of customs and folklore!* At the same time (this was the second half of the 1980s) I came upon verbal traditions among North American shamans that emphatically recommended the cleansing of crystals on that *subtle* level by laying them in an Amethyst druse.

I set about verifying the findings. Healing crystals that had been applied to people with serious illnesses were tested by sensitive persons, who usually reported unpleasant sensations. Naturally, I was sceptical enough to mix in 'unused' crystals among the tested ones; but, to my astonishment, these were in fact perceived as 'more neutral'. The obviously 'polluted' crystals were then subjected to various cleansing methods; they were sprinkled with salt, held in the smoke of burning incense, and laid on pieces of Amethyst druse. Lo and behold, afterwards those crystals triggered neither unpleasant sensations nor any kind of symptoms of illness. Even the Heliotrope we mentioned at the beginning was 'clean' again.

Ever since then, the cleansing of crystals has become standard practice for the safe and careful handling of healing crystals. Undesirable 'side effects' can thus be clearly reduced, and the successful application of healing crystals becomes more reliable.

Also, interesting insights about 'cleansing and protection' as applied to human beings themselves were gleaned from our experiences with the crystals; this little book reports these as well.

Tübingen, Spring 2008
Michael Gienger

---

* Hanns Bächtold-Stäubli, *Handwoerterbuch des deutschen Aberglaubens* [Handbook on German Superstitions], (Reprint of the original edition of 1936), Berlin, Walter de Gruyter Verlag, 1987.

How Do Crystals Become Contaminated?

Invisible Ballast

Have you ever experienced the following: You catch sight of a beautiful crystal, but when you pick it up it feels strange? Or, you wear you favourite crystal necklace, but after a while it feels as heavy as lead and tight around your neck? What you are perceiving is the 'invisible ballast', which has become 'attached' to the crystal. But what is it?

The invisible ballast is simply absorbed and stored 'information'. In itself, this absorption and storage of information is nothing negative at all. Only if it begins to disturb us and affect us negatively do we perceive it as 'ballast'. Otherwise, the information is simply *there*...

The most impressive experience I have had in connection with this subject was with a piece of East Prussian Amber from an old collection. When I held the piece in my hand for the first time, I had the sudden impulse to close my eyes and I then saw in front of me a broad expanse of landscape with rippling fields of grain. I expressed these impressions in words for those present, and when I opened my eyes an old lady standing nearby with tears in her eyes said, 'You have just described my old home with beautiful words!' She came from East Prussia and had instantly recognized the landscape I had described – but the thing was, I had never been to East Prussia. This meant that the vision could only have been conjured up by the piece of Amber. This touched me so deeply that, ever since, I have had a strong desire to travel to the Baltic region. Afterwards, by 'coincidence', I came across, among others, books such as *Die Mücke im Bernstein* (The Gnat in Amber),* a novel about East Prussia.

Naturally, this was an example neither of 'ballast' nor of 'contamination', as the information from the piece of Amber touched me in a very

* Else G. Stahl, *Die Mücke im Bernstein*, Munich, Franz Ehrenwirth Verlag, 1971, (paperback: Lübbe Tb. No. 12952, Bergisch Gladbach 1989).

positive and inspiring way. But it shows precisely the two sides of the same coin: where we come across beautiful or pleasant information, we are attracted to it; on the other hand, where we encounter burdening or debilitating information, we are repelled by it. This value judgement of 'attractive' or 'repulsive' is made by no one but ourselves! Just think of music (also a kind of information); what one person likes is perceived as awful by another.

But, just as we can turn off music we dislike (at least we can if it is coming from our own radio), we can also eliminate disturbing information from crystals, providing it is not the crystal's 'own' information deriving from its colour, composition, structure or its creative origin.* Those types of information are essential characteristics of that crystal and cannot be removed! But, what is 'information' really?

Information

To understand the nature of 'information' we can use the example of our thoughts: Thoughts are not material things (they are not graspable), and they are not a physical energy form (no measuring instrument can detect them). However, thoughts can be perceived and exchanged. Have you ever had the experience that you 'had a thought', and then somebody else verbalized that exact thought?

Pieces of information are mental ideas and concepts. They are ideas about *how something is*, or concepts about *how something functions*. Even the classical philosophers, such as Socrates, Plato and Aristotle, spoke about the 'world of ideas' behind the 'world of manifest things'. All of nature is organized through an exchange of information. Sounds, images and thoughts are *pieces of information*, which we create ourselves, or absorb, and pass on. Matter, too, is shaped and formed through information, as Rupert Sheldrake's research has shown.**

* see Michael Gienger, *Crystal Power, Crystal Healing*, London, Cassell, 1998.
** Rupert Sheldrake, *The New Science of Life (The Hypothesis of Formative Causation)*, London, Paladin, 1987.

So, information in itself is something intangible and neither energy nor matter. There is often confusion about these things. Very often, energy in particular is equated with information. But they are really two different things. The best way to understand this is through the example of a radio transmitter: a radio will transmit energy at a very particular frequency; in order to receive the transmission we adjust our radio sets to the same frequency (x number of megahertz). Thus, through 'resonance' (a shared vibration at the same frequency), we have established an energetic connection. From then on we can receive the information that the radio transmitter sends through modulations (variations in intensity or interruptions) with its 'transmitting energy'. But, in the end, what we hear from our radios is not the transmission frequency itself (that would only sound as one note), but rather the information that is transported by means of the frequency, like a rider on horseback.

This means that information can be stored on energy and then be 'read' or retrieved from the energy (examples: radio transmitters, television transmitters, radio waves, mobile phones, etc.). What we actually receive, perceive and work with is not the carrier frequency (energy), but the stored information. The same applies to material storage of information. The letters of the alphabet, which you are reading at this moment, consist simply of black particles on white paper. What you are absorbing and working with is not the paper and the printer's ink (at least I hope you are not eating this little booklet!), but essentially the information 'stored' upon it.

Attachment

What is attachment? It is the way in which information can be 'attached' to energy or matter, without *being* the energy or matter. However, the 'attached information' will alter its carrier. Thus a printed page may make a person laugh (if you read it and don't eat it!) or even cause one to feel deeply depressed (some novels might just as well be printed straight onto tissues!), something a piece of white paper cannot possibly do. Attached information may therefore massively overlie the carrier medium and change it.

Attachment is something we experience on a daily basis. In the field of crystal healing it happens particularly when we perceive something 'quite different' about a crystal that initially comes across as simply a thing of beauty; such as, a sensation, a feeling, a perception, an inspiration, an idea, or similar. It may be part of the crystal itself, because the colour, the composition, the structure and the origin of the crystal provide perceptible information; however, it may simply be something 'attached' to the crystal that has nothing at all to do with the crystal itself. This is similar to water, in which foreign influences can even become visible in its movement, when it dries, or is frozen;* thus, thoughts, feelings, moods, or even information about illnesses can become 'attached' to the crystal, to energy, or to matter, and thereby become connected with it.

The crystallization of ice can cause stored information to become visible.

* see M. Gienger/J. Goebel, *Gem Water*, Earthdancer/Findhorn, 2008.

Information stored in crystals is definitely perceptible! One can feel whether the person who polished the crystal or worked on it had a good or a bad day, whether the previous wearer of a piece of jewellery was well or sick. American Indian shamans also call crystals 'holders of energy', as crystals store such information particularly well (as compared with water) and for a very long time. Quartz crystals in particular are therefore called by shamans the 'memory cells of the Earth'.

Cleansing

It is precisely this 'attached' foreign information in crystals that may become 'invisible ballast' if it triggers unpleasant sensations and reactions in us. Or it may even trigger symptoms of an illness, thus interfering with and impairing our physical and mental functions.

In such cases we can use methods for 'cleansing' crystals, that is, liberating them from this 'invisible ballast'. The following pages provide various procedures for 'cleansing' crystals, methods that have been tried and tested on many occasions and are certainly effective. Pay attention to this aspect of the care of your crystals so that beyond being pleasing to look at, they are also able to bring about wellbeing.

Washing and Cleansing Crystals

Before we proceed to cleansing crystals on a subtle, vibrational level, let us first take a look at the cleansing of crystals in the everyday sense of the word. Crystals used for massage should obviously be cleaned for hygienic reasons, and have oil, perspiration and skin particles removed from them; but also jewellery, or other crystals that are worn externally, should be thoroughly cleaned on a regular basis, and washed if necessary.

Contamination and Changes

Contact with perspiration and oils from human skin, or even sometimes simple contact with humidity and oxygen, can cause changes in the surface of some crystals. Deposits may form (oils from skin, etc.), especially on jewellery or on porous and therefore absorbent crystals. Chemical changes may occur on the surface (through perspiration, air humidity or oxygen), or the wax or oil may be lost with which the crystal was treated to improve its brilliance or transparency.

Such influences may cause a crystal to change. Its brilliance may fade (with Hematite, for example); its surface may look dull (Purpurite); metal settings may discolour (especially silver), etc. These changes may impair the beauty of the crystal quite considerably, which, in turn, may lead to a change in our internal attitude towards the crystal; ultimately we make our own personal decisions about what disturbs us and what does not.

Looked at objectively, the healing effect of a crystal does not change if it merely loses a little transparency, brilliance or colour on the surface.

11

However, a crystal that no longer pleases us the way it once did will automatically be worn or applied less often, which could considerably impair its effect. It follows, then, that washing and cleaning crystals is not simply an aesthetic or hygienic matter, but also a regular renewing and encouraging of our positive 'tuning in' to the crystal in question.

Changes in a crystal can occur, however, that cannot be reversed through washing or cleansing; for example, changes in the surface of the crystal through chemical transformations. Other changes can even be exacerbated, for example a dulling effect, through removing oil and wax. Please be assured in such cases that the effectiveness of the crystal still remains the same afterwards. Claims that the crystal would then become useless and value-less are simply wrong! Think about how you previously used the crystal (as jewellery and/or as a healing crystal), and consider that they are worth looking after and applying for that reason alone.

Cleansing and Washing

Particularly in the following cases, healing crystals should be very thoroughly cleansed and, if necessary, washed:

- Newly purchased crystals, before they are applied for the first time.
- Visibly dirty or superficially changed crystals.
- Crystals used for massage – after their application, or after they have been worn on the body for an extended period of time.
- Crystals that have been lent to someone and were used by them for application with illnesses.

Mechanical cleansing through thorough washing and, if necessary, scrubbing, is the first step in such cases – until the crystal is really clean. If the contamination is severe, maybe even use an ecological washing up liquid, or a washing lotion (described below), or a medium for cleaning jewellery. Afterwards, thoroughly rinse the crystals under running, hand-warm water!

Mechanical cleansing   *Disinfecting*

When scrubbing or washing a crystal, please take into account the natural sensitivity of the crystal type. Filigree or brittle minerals should be cleansed very carefully and thoroughly, maybe only with an artist's paintbrush.

It goes without saying that water soluble crystals should never be washed or held under water. Water soluble crystals include some of the more frequently used healing crystals, for example: Alum, Chalcanthite (copper vitriol), Halite and Ulexite. Others are sensitive to water or washing solutions: Purpurite, Pyrite, Galenite and other sulphides (salts of sulphur). In the case of Noble Opal, many cleansing agents should be avoided altogether as they may well change the content of water in the crystal, water being most important for the opalizing effect!

After cleansing and washing, crystals may be disinfected with alcohol, which is especially useful before employing the crystal to make gem water* or for hygienic reasons during applications for massage. The best

---

* M. Gienger/J. Goebel, *Gem Water*, Earthdancer/Findhorn, 2008.

way is to rub the crystals with a clean cloth moistened with alcohol and then rinse them under running water. Complete immersion in high percentage grade alcohol would only damage some types of crystals. And, naturally, the crystals mentioned above that are water-soluble, or sensitive to water, must be exempted from such treatment altogether!

A Patented Cleansing Lotion

In order to thoroughly cleanse crystals used for massage or therapy, before and after application, and also to cleanse the crystals on a subtle level, Monika Grundmann, founder of 'Crystal Balance',* developed a washing lotion that works on deep levels and is energetically balanced. With a background in crystal healing massage, as well as being a cosmetician/beautician, Monika spent a long time looking for a comprehensive cleansing system for herself and for the materials she works with. Physical cleanliness and spiritual hygiene were both to be taken into consideration. The goal was refreshment and cleansing on all levels. Ultimately, she was able to develop an effective lotion consisting of organic coconut soap for the physical cleansing; scented oils, such as orange oil and incense for cleansing, disinfecting and psychic refreshment; and spagyric Amethyst essence for mental clearing. The result is a comprehensive and holistically effective washing lotion, which is just as suitable for personal body-care and as a 'balm for the soul' as for cleansing crystals, massage beds, treatment rooms and more.

Particularly suitable for crystals that are employed for massage or bodywork, and for healing crystals that are used intensively, this washing lotion is an outstanding product. The Frankincense and Amethyst essences in the lotion also eliminate a great deal of foreign information.

* see also Monika Grundmann, *Crystal Balance*, Earthdancer/Findhorn, 2008, as well as www.crystal-balance.com

Important facts about the cleansing lotion:

- **Area of application:** Massage crystals, healing crystals with body contact, treatment rooms and utensils, as well as for holistic body care.
- **Application:** Use as you would a soap, or other cleansing material.
- **Not suitable for:** Sensitive mineral clusters; crystals that are water-soluble (Chalcanthite; Halite, etc.); or for crystal necklaces, as the string might be affected and break.

Cleaning Jewellery

The cleaning of a piece jewellery is particularly important if deposits of dirt and oil from skin have formed, for example, in the setting – but it can be quite tricky if the crystal and its setting have different degrees of sensitivity. Thus many a Turquoise has not survived being immersed in a 'silver bath' and, by contrast, some silver settings will discolour even faster if they are cleaned with water or cleansing solutions. In such cases, naturally, one has to be very careful, and cleansing by experts (goldsmiths, jewellers) is recommended; they will use ultrasound cleansing devices and similar options not found in an ordinary household.

In less complicated cases, jewellery can, of course, be cleaned at home. A whole range of appropriate cleaning agents are available in the trade, of which we introduce here, as examples, two products offered by a company called Sambol* suitable for cleaning pieces of jewellery with crystals/gems in settings, and precious metals. The products have been tested and, with proper usage, are completely harmless:

Jewellery Cleaner by Sambol: A gentle cleansing agent for jewellery with gems in settings, which removes fat and dirt from jewellery that has been worn, as well as removing the remains of the grinding and polishing

* see also www.sambol.de

15

pastes used during the preparation of the jewellery. The great advantage of this product is that it is suitable for all types of jewellery, and it will not damage soft or sensitive crystals.

Amber Clean by Sambol: Particularly helpful in cleaning and de-oxidizing silver jewellery. By contrast with other silver immersion baths, it protects soft crystal. (However, not suitable for use with mother-of-pearl.) *Amber Clean* is extremely effective! For this reason, immerse jewellery with gems or crystals only very briefly, then very thoroughly rinse under lukewarm running water and dry.

You will find further cleaning/cleansing agents, silver immersion baths, polish for precious metals, and sprays for protecting against discoloration in the specialist trade. Please also ask for information about the application in question as well as about which crystals/gems the cleansing agents are suitable for. We have purposely chosen only two agents for inclusion in this booklet; with proper use they will not harm any decorative crystal/gem.

The most important points to remember:
- **Use for:** Jewellery made of precious metals with or without gems in settings.
- **Application:** Use as you would a soap, or other cleansing material.
- **Not suitable for:** Sensitive mineral clusters and water soluble crystals (Chalcanthite; Halite, etc.); do not use Amber Clean for jewellery made with mother-of-pearl.

Now that we have looked at *external* cleansing, let us turn our attention to *internal* cleansing, which consists of two important steps: *Dis-charging*, and cleansing on a subtle level.

Discharging

Energy as an Information Carrier

Crystals absorb energy. They become warm if they are held in one's hand or worn against the body, or even hot if they are placed in the sun. Part of the information that we sense as 'invisible ballast' is connected with this absorbed energy. For example, if a crystal is worn when the wearer is ill, often it will quickly become hot, even if there is no fever present. Along with this energy that we can feel, information about the illness is also stored in the crystal: information about one's physical state (pain, symptoms of the illness), about one's moods (unhappiness, grief, etc.), and about one's thoughts (anxieties, thoughts about the illness, or about getting better) may all be connected with the energy absorbed.

Discharging Energies

In order to release this energy and the information connected with it, the crystals should be regularly discharged. The best time is always when they are taken off (for example, before going to bed) or whenever they 'feel unpleasant' to us.

The best method for discharging crystals is to hold them under running water. Water absorbs energy (warmth, static charges, etc.) and then allows it to flow away. With the energy disappears part of the foreign information connected with it.

Hold the crystal you wish to discharge under running water for at least one minute, while (if possible) vigorously rubbing the surface of the crystal with your fingers. To begin with, the surface will often feel 'soapy', so that your fingers glide smoothly across it. Gradually, resistance from the surface becomes greater and the movement of your fingers across the surface is 'braked'. This indicates that the crystal has been discharged.

The most important points about discharging:
- **Application:** Before using the crystal for the first time, as well as after using or wearing it – or whenever you feel it is necessary!
- **Duration:** For at least one minute under running (lukewarm or cold) water.
- **Unsuitable for:** Sensitive mineral clusters, water-soluble crystals (Chalcanthite, Halite, etc.), and crystal pendants or necklaces (see below).
- **Tip:** While discharging, breathe out vigorously so that you yourself do not absorb energy and information.

Necklaces with crystals should only be cleansed with a damp cloth, as the strings may otherwise deteriorate or break. Take the damp cloth in one hand and pull the necklace through the cloth several times. This, too, will discharge the crystals. Afterwards rinse out the cloth and thoroughly wash your hands under running water, otherwise there is a risk of personally absorbing the discharged energy.

Discharging on Hematite?

It is often recommended to discharge crystals by placing them on top of small tumbled Hematite crystals. It is true that Hematite is able to allow energy to flow away because of its good conductibility (which is why the crystal often feels cold to the touch); however, this effect is in no way as comprehensive as with running water. In addition, the small tumbled Hematite crystals will often absorb energy themselves and will then have to be cleansed as well. Instead of having just one crystal that needs cleansing, you suddenly have many! Thus the Hematite method is problematic as compared with running water; the method is also much more involved.

Discharging in a Freezer Compartment?

Another method recommended in some literature for discharging crystals is storing them in the freezer compartment of your fridge. Through the cooling-down process the crystals do actually discharge energy, which is why, shortly after taking them out of the compartment, they do feel 'fresher'. However, the effect is only short-lived. As soon as the crystal is warmed up to room temperature, the previous state (along with the associated feeling) will return. In addition, one will also find that none of the foreign information was eliminated (as compared with water, which allows information attached to the energies to flow away). On the contrary, the cold temperature has more of a conserving effect on information. In the case of some devices, the surrounding electromagnetic 'smog' even causes additional information to be added! For this reason the method is, in the end, most unsatisfactory.

So far, the best and unchallenged method for discharging information from crystals is running water. However, with this method too, the discharging process will only eliminate part of the absorbed foreign information from the crystal. Thus, further steps for cleansing should be carried out.

Cleansing

Transience Information

A truly, deeply effective cleansing of crystals on a subtle level will be accomplished if one succeeds in dissolving the attached information and in completely eliminating it. Methods that bring this about, however varied or different they may be from each other, always have one thing in common – they transmit information regarding transience.

From a spiritual point of view, 'transience' is the opposite of 'attachment'. If the transience of things is truly recognized, there is nothing left to attach or hold onto; instead there is an opportunity to let go and to experience true liberation.

This realization, which we humans may experience during meditation, is obviously valid for all levels of being. Whenever this *transience information* comes into play, dissolving and liberating processes begin. Amethyst contains this transience information through the influence of radioactive radiation during its creation, which also gives it its violet colour. During the process of cleansing crystals with frankincense, the crystals derive this transience information from the burning of the incense; and from the intense vibrations of singing bowls, which can cause structures to resonate and even dissolve. Salt, as a deeply cleansing medium, contains this information in several forms: in salt is united information from a strong acid *and* from a strong alkaline medium (hydrochloric acid and caustic soda/sodium hydroxide), both substances that have great power to dissolve. And even though the ions in salt attract each other with great force, salt will still dissolve very rapidly in water – it virtually disappears into 'nothing'... This *transience information* then leads to the dissolving of other information from its attachment to the carrier medium (energy or matter) and its previous 'content' disappears.

What is perceptible in that moment of deep cleansing is the release of neutral energy, or simply a sense of complete and utter liberation. These sensations confirm that a comprehensive cleansing has actually taken place.

Now for the most important methods, in detail:

Cleansing on Amethyst

Amethyst triggers the ability to dissolve 'attachments'. We experience this immediately when Amethyst helps us to let go of sadness and grief and to find inner peace; or when it helps us to let go of addictions and cravings in order to become freer and more self-determining.

Amethyst's *cleansing information* says, 'Put an end to attachment and liberate yourself from all attachments!' This applies both to ourselves, if we are holding onto something too doggedly, as well as to that which attaches itself too tightly to us. Amethyst brings liberation and is therefore highly prized among orders of monks in many religions. Not for nothing can it be seen adorning the finger-rings of Catholic bishops.

Amethyst works for animals as well (the dissolving of traumatic experiences), plants (driving away pests), and even crystals. It is precisely this *cleansing information* that causes Amethyst to liberate crystals of all types from attached foreign information. Because it dissolves the 'attachment', it does not matter which foreign information it is, or which crystal is involved.

When cleansing using Amethyst, the crystals in question need simply to be laid in an Amethyst druse or on a piece of Amethyst druse. The energy radiating from the tips of the Amethyst crystals penetrates the crystal lying on top of it (or in it) with the so-called *cleansing information*, so that all foreign information is dissolved. If the crystals were held under running water to discharge them beforehand, two or three hours with Amethyst will suffice. If that is not possible (for example with necklaces of crystals), eight to twelve hours is a necessary minimum. It may even be carried out for longer as there is no such thing as *too much* in this case.

The most important points about cleansing with Amethyst:
- **Application:** Before using the crystal for the first time, as well as every time it is taken off – or whenever it feels necessary!
- **Duration:** After previous discharging, two to three hours; otherwise eight to twelve hours, preferably even longer.
- **Suitable for:** All crystals except Amber (see below).

Cleansing in Salt

Salt is a substance whose cleansing and purifying effects have been highly prized in all cultures and at all times. Salt has been employed for thousands of years to banish negative influences, to divert conflict, and to heal illnesses, all of which is nothing other than liberation from 'attached' information (see 'Transience Information' above).

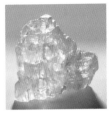

Salt has this quality because it has, in itself, been created through a long cleansing and purifying process. In addition, as a cubic mineral, it has a crystal structure of the highest order, as well as a very balanced composition; an acid and an alkaline substance are united in salt in a ratio of exactly 1:1. It is thanks to these factors that salt is able to cleanse on an even deeper level and faster even than Amethyst. Its information simply reads, 'Cleanse and purify yourself!'.

In order to cleanse crystals with this method, lay them in salt crystals, rock salt or sea salt. Nothing else needs to be done as the information from the salt has a deeply penetrating effect. Even after an hour or two the crystals will be completely cleansed. But they should not be left for more than three to four hours or the salt will have an energetically exhausting effect. Please observe this carefully (set an alarm clock!).

Great care must be taken when using salt water! It is occasionally recommended as salt water has a similar cleansing effect to dry salt. However, salt water attacks many crystals chemically!

The consequences may extend from making the surface look dull or cloudy (salt crystallization in cracks and pores in the crystal) and heightened porosity, right through to partial decomposition of the mineral substance. Just remember what salt water does to our cars in winter! Therefore, salt water – if used at all – should only be employed with hard, chemically resistant crystals. And please take special care with recipes in which salt water is supposed to have vinegar added to it. The acid in the vinegar will simply make the mixture even more aggressive!

In some cases, even dry salt in direct contact with some crystals may lead to dulling of the crystal's surface or to drying out (take care with opals!), so for safety's sake the crystals should be placed in small glass dishes which, in turn, are embedded in larger dishes of salt (see illustration). The effect of the salt will penetrate the glass. Likewise, white cloths may be placed over the dishes of salt and the crystals then bedded on top of the cloth. The salt will still have a sufficiently penetrating effect.

Cleansing with salt is recommended especially when the foreign information turns out to be particularly 'persistent', i.e. cannot be dissolved and eliminated with any of the other methods. The only crystal, so far, that has turned out to be resistant against cleansing with salt is Amber (see below).

The most important points about cleansing with salt:
- **Application:** For particularly persistent information (when other methods do not work).
- **Duration:** One to two, at most three to four hours!
- **Suitability:** All crystals except Amber (see below). However, for the sake of keeping the crystals safe, they should be protected from direct contact with salt through using small glass dishes or cloths (see above).

Cleansing in Sunlight

The midday sun at its highest point and fullest strength has a cleansing effect that can dissolve and wipe away foreign information. This is due to the higher intensity of UV radiation around midday. Sunlight at both sunrise and sunset, shortly after rising or shortly before setting, with its higher proportion of light in the red part of the spectrum, will actually be more inclined to *charge* the crystal.

This cleansing method is, however, not recommended, as the crystal may lose some of its colour in direct sunlight (Amethyst, Fluorite, Rose Quartz and others) or may even completely decompose (Realgar).

Gems (crystals) and minerals originate in darkness in the Earth, which is why the colour of some crystals may be unstable in the comparatively stronger influence of sunlight. However, there is a single 'crystal' for which this method is the only one that works – Amber!

Amber is a fossil resin. Information will be anchored more firmly in its organic substance than in other 'mineral' crystals. This is why, interestingly enough, Amethyst and salt will do very little to cleanse Amber. Burning incense and using singing bowls will accomplish a little more, but still not cleanse sufficiently. The best means of cleansing Amber is to place it in the light of the midday sun; however, even that has to be allowed to work over longer periods, again and again, until a comprehensive cleansing process has taken place. So the best approach is to hold Amber once daily, for several days, under running water, in order to discharge it, and then afterwards lay it in the midday sun. In this manner, foreign information can be removed, for the most part, even from Amber.

The most important points about cleansing in sunlight:

- **Application:** Mainly for Amber, as well as for other sunlight-resistant crystals.
- **Duration:** Three to four hours around the midday period; even longer for Amber, repeating the procedure for several days in a row!
- **Suitable for** minerals with their own intrinsic coloration (idiochromatic). Minerals with 'borrowed' colour (allochromatic minerals) may, in certain circumstances, become paler.*

Cleansing with Incense and Singing Bowls

Both the burning of incense and the harmonic vibrations of singing bowls can also dissolve 'attached' information. The application of both methods,

often in combination, is counted among the traditional customs in many cultures for the purification of objects, rooms, the aura, and the body. Thus the burning of incense and the vibrations of singing bowls can also be used for crystals.

Certain herbs, types of wood and resins possess a special purifying power. They are, among others, Frankincense (Olibanum), Dammar Gum, Guggul (Indian myrrh) and Juniper (the German meaning being *lively, evergreen tree*).**

---

* Minerals with their own intrinsic colours consist of essential parts of colouring elements. Minerals with 'foreign' colouring, on the other hand, derive their colours from trace elements, impurities, crystal lattice effects, free electrons, or similar. This makes the latter more susceptible to the influence of radiation.

** From Old German *wachal* = 'awake, fresh, life-preserving' and *tar* = 'tree'. The parts used are the tips of shoots.

A very effective incense mixture for the purification of crystals has been created out of the above ingredients and a little Himalaya salt. When strewn on a piece of charcoal, the mixture develops a deep, resinous-woody aroma. If the crystals are held in the rising smoke for two to three minutes, the stored foreign information is dissolved. The cleansing incense mixture can be obtained in specialist shops.

Singing bowls have a similar effect on a crystal when it is laid in the bowl. The intense vibrations of the sound are able to cleanse a crystal within two to three minutes, if the bowl is tapped in a quiet rhythm or is incited to produce a constant note through rubbing the rim of the bowl with a wooden implement. The size and the note of the bowl appear not to be a deciding factor in the effectiveness of the method. Larger crystals that cannot fit into a singing bowl can be cleansed by moving the vibrating bowl around them several times.

The most important points about cleansing with incense or with singing bowls:
- **Application:** Before using a crystal for the first time, as well as when a crystal is removed after wearing it – or whenever you feel it is necessary!
- **Duration:** Two to three minutes; longer for Amber or stubbornly persistent information!
- **Suitability:** All crystals (but will not always work for Amber!).
- **Tip:** Ideal in connection with mental support during a purification ritual (see below).

The Cleansing Ritual

The effects of burning incense and of using sounds, as well as, in principle, the effects of all discharging and cleansing methods, can be intensified and deepened if the cleansing process is carried out as a consciously conducted ritual and the cleansing process is supported by consciously holding the intention to cleanse.

Whatever the cleansing method (burning incense, tapping the singing bowl, placing a crystal on Amethyst, etc.), we 'insert' the mental intention that all information not belonging to the crystal should return to its origin or be liberated. Conscious intention also makes it easier to dissolve strong attachments.

'Foreign' information is not 'bad' in itself. It is only irritating if its attachment means that the qualities of a crystal (or other things) are overlain or if they are blocked. If the information returns to its real origin, or dissolves out of any kind of attachment state, it becomes free for a purposeful function within the Universe. This shamanic viewpoint, which may be unusual for us, has perceptible effects when cleansing crystals. Try it out, and make the tedious duty of cleansing your crystals into a conscious ritual act of liberation. This will really do something positive for your crystals – and for you as well! More on this in the following chapter.

The Cleansing Ceremony

The most effective and beautiful way to carry out the cleansing of crystals is with a ceremony that is conducted with full awareness and attention. This cleansing process will acquire a very special quality through our heart-felt attention to the crystals.

Preparation

Before beginning the ceremony, we should physically tidy the space where it is to be held and prepare a pleasant place for the cleansing work. A cleansing ceremony in the middle of a pile of junk will just not work....

After preparing the space, cleanse yourself by washing or showering (using the cleansing lotion would be a good idea!). I recommend wearing light-coloured, comfortable clothing, if possible made of natural fibres; take off any metal objects, such as mobile phones, watches, metal jewellery, rings, etc. Providing you find it comfortable, go barefoot; roll up your sleeves, or wear clothing with short sleeves. In all cases, ensure that external disturbances are eliminated: unplug the telephone, switch off music and the television. A ceremony requires one's undivided attention!

'Pre-cleanse' the crystals as well by physically cleaning them and washing them with the cleansing lotion. If necessary, clean waxed crystals with alcohol (for subsequent gem water preparation or similar). After that, we should not touch the crystals with our hands anymore. It is preferable to move them around using wooden tongs, or by laying them on cloths.

Collection

Collecting the items to be used for the ceremony can be part of the phase of 'collecting oneself', and, in doing so, a sense of inner calm and focus can begin to arise within you. You could also meditate as part of your preparation, and exercises for focussing attention are also highly recommended.

When a focussed and attentive state of mind has been achieved, you can prepare the items for the ceremony: flowers as an offering, pure water (perhaps from a special spring or well, or water that has been specially blessed) mixed with a little crystallized salt, incense sticks, a singing bowl or bell, an incense burner and the cleansing incense mixture, a candle, and matches or a lighter.

All the items should be set out pleasingly, the flowers laid out and the incense sticks lit. This burning of incense before beginning the ceremony is a supportive measure; it lifts the energetic level of the room and sets the stage for the ceremony.

Ceremony

The ceremony begins as you bring your full awareness to the lighting of the candle. The essential factor is your intention, which is released to the universe at the moment of lighting the candle. You could, for example, ask for support with the cleansing process and silently ask for the release of all attached information. The cleansing process should be beneficial to all those who later handle or apply the crystals. Sprinkling them with pure water as a way of giving thanks for any support received also further raises the power of the ceremony.

Next, the washed and dried crystals are laid out – in the form of a mandala, if desired. After that, we 'rinse' them with sound. The ringing of the singing bowl or bell is conducted with slow movements over the crystals, so that they are virtually 'bathed in the sound'.

Light the charcoal in a fire-proof incense burner; allow the charcoal to glow and turn ashy, then sprinkle on some incense, equivalent to the size of a pea.

When the smoke begins to rise, slowly move the crystals through the smoke, or fan the smoke across the crystals, with a feather for example.

Then, following your inner voice, with thankfulness complete the ceremony, using sound, song or a quiet prayer. During this part, we have another opportunity to use our minds to release any attached information so that it may return back to its origins or be liberated.

Closing the Ceremony

After having carried out the ceremony, thoroughly air the room and then lay the crystals inside an Amethyst druse. Any small crystals of the same type may be assembled in a small cotton bag and laid in the druse.

The flowers used in the ceremony should be given back to Nature. This, too, should be done with respect and thankfulness.

When everything has been cleared away, we can mentally end the ceremony by turning our attention to other things once more.

The Course of the Ceremony

Preparation
- (Choose a time and place where you will not be disturbed)
- Pre-cleansing the crystals (scrubbing and washing)
- Preparing the space
- Cleansing yourself

Collection
- Meditation (focussing exercises)
- Gathering the items for the ceremony:
  *Flowers as an offering – Pure water with a little crystallized salt –
  Incense sticks – A singing bowl or bell – Incense burner –
  Cleansing incense mixture – Candle*
- Lighting the incense

Ceremony
- Focussed lighting of the candle
- Laying out the crystals
- Bathing the crystals in sound
- Cleansing the crystals in the incense smoke
- Continuing the ceremony with sound, song, or silent devotion
- Using the mind to release and liberate information

Closing
- Airing the room
- Final cleansing in the Amethyst druse
- Returning the flowers to Nature
- Clearing away
- Turning one's attention to other things

Charging

Amplifying and Awakening Your Crystals

If a particularly intense application of healing crystals is called for, or a very rapid effect is required, it makes sense not only to cleanse them before using them, but also to 'charge them up'. Charging is a process of activating the healing properties of crystals by raising the energy levels in them. All energy conducted into a crystal is also passed on again by the crystal, thus adding to its radiating effect. This is comparable to a radio transmitter: output is raised by adding extra electrical power that, in turn, makes its radiating effect more powerful and far-reaching.

On the physical plain, any kind of warming of the crystal already signi-fies a form of charging up.

Ambient warmth, sunlight or body heat will transfer new energy to a crystal; electro-magnetic radiation and sound waves of the subtlest kind are created, which the crystal then uses to transmit its own information to its surroundings.

An additional effect is perceived on the 'subtle level'. Crystals actually experience a rhythmic alternation of rest and activity on their molecular level. Dowsing trials demonstrate a clear change in the energy potential within crystals during the course of a day, a year, or during the Moon cycle.* Even if the physically quantifiable amount of energy given off by the crystal appears to be the same, it still does not manifest the same *quality* of energy at all times. Charging up the crystal therefore not only changes the quantity of the energy given off, but also its quality.

By charging up a crystal, the crystal is 'woken up', so to speak – the intrinsic characteristics are activated and raised into a higher state of 'effective readiness'.

This can be compared with reading out a text: even if we read out the text at the same speed and volume, there will be a difference, depending on whether we happen to be dreadfully tired or wide awake. This difference will also be transmitted to the listeners.

Thus two different effects belong to the act of charging up crystals. On the one hand, there is a raising of the radiating effect through adding energy (light and heat); on the other hand, there is the awakening of the crystal on the subtle level, which then activates it and places it in a state of 'effective readiness'.

Traditional Methods

The charging up of crystals has its roots in shamanism. Before being used, the healing crystals are 'woken up' and activated through burning incense, singing, warming them in one's hands, blowing across them in short and intense bursts, holding them on particular chakras (energy centres), and through other ritual acts. Mental support of their effect also plays a big role: the crystals are often 'awakened' in one's thoughts, or

* 'Radiesthesis' means 'perception of radiation' (Lat. *radius* = 'ray' and Gr. *aisthesis* = 'perception, sensitivity, ability to feel or sense'). Radiesthetic (dowsing) tests are carried out with pendulums, dowsing rods, or similar devices. Literature on this: Rainer Strebel/Michael Gienger, *Die Individuelle Therapie* [Individual Therapy], Baden (CH), AT Verlag, 2004.

'reminded' of their task. This awakening of the crystals is also well known in the European traditions surrounding the knowledge of healing crystals, and can be found, among other places, in the instructions handed down by Hildegard von Bingen.*

Modern Methods

As ritual elements are often met with incomprehension nowadays, modern methods of charging up crystals take a more technical approach. Warming the crystals is the most commonly used method as it has the added advantage of making the crystals feel more pleasant when applied to the body. In the professional sphere, the crystals are warmed by laying them in a bed of sand, in warm water, or even in warmed massage oil.

At home, simply place the crystals in a dish on the radiator, in a warm place. However, we do not recommend warming them with an electrical device (stove, oven, microwave oven) as many electrical devices can change the information within the crystal and alter its effectiveness due to ambient electromagnetic smog. Warm water (central heating) and flames (wood burner, candles) are preferable. Of course, crystals can simply be warmed up in one's hands, or by wearing them close to one's body. This, too, wakes up and activates the crystals.

Charging Crystals in Sunlight

A very pleasant method of awakening and activating crystals is by charging them in the light of the morning or evening sun. The crystals should be placed in the light at sunrise or sunset in such a way that they are completely enveloped in the red-gold sunlight.

When the sun is sitting just above the horizon, its light has a wonderful charging quality – at just about the time when one can actually look at the sun with the naked eye. For the purpose of charging crystals, they should not be in the sunlight for much longer than that red-gold period, then they should be brought back into the house or to a shady place.

At midday the nature of the sunlight is more dis-charging because of the higher degree of UV rays and the lesser degree of light from the red end of the spectrum. Therefore it follows that the timeframe for charging the crystal is for about half an hour after sunrise or half an hour before sunset. These timeframes are applicable for the temperate climate zone. In the tropics and sub-tropics this charging period is shortened because of the rapid sunrise and sunset; in sub-polar regions it can be quite a bit longer.

Charging Crystals in Moonlight

There are many references to be found regarding the charging of crystals in moonlight, especially at Full Moon. For this purpose, the crystals are laid in moonlight, in the night, in such a way that they are completely enveloped in the silvery light of the Moon. However, it should be noted that moonlight holds intrinsic information to a far higher degree than sunlight. Moonlight not only raises the intrinsic information within the crystals, but also adds new qualities to them.

Charging up crystals in moonlight is suitable, in the first instance, for healing crystals that are used in applications for the water balance in the body (body fluids; lymph; blood; urinary tract system; hormonal system; immune system; and similar). Crystals of this nature often display a much stronger effect through being charged in moonlight.

It should be noted that moonlight demonstrates perceptibly different qualities during the various phases of the Moon. The phases of the waxing Moon, including Full Moon, are more suitable for 'building up' processes, which will strengthen existing qualities and increase them. During the waning Moon, it is the dissolving and cleansing processes that are emphasized, thus also the curing of illnesses. The light of the waxing Moon has a tendency towards a charging nature, while the waning Moon is more dis-charging in nature.

The most important points for charging crystals in moonlight:
- **Application:** After finishing a cleansing ceremony.
- **Time:** At night, in full moonlight, for processes of increase during the waxing phase, for dissolving or cleansing processes during the waning phase.
- **Suitable for:** Especially those crystals that have a connection with the systems of fluids in the body.

Charging on Rock Crystal

The most preferred method in the crystal healing world is charging up crystals on Rock Crystal. Rock Crystal is a neutral quartz (only if it too has been cleansed!), which consistently supports and fortifies the existing state of being. Its qualities of clarity, purity and consciousness can thus also awaken other crystals, activate them, and enhance their expression.

Quartz crystals, such as Rock Crystal or Amethyst, also have the characteristic of absorbing energy through their base or sides and then releasing it in a concentrated form through their tips. This can even be physically measured: the heat conductivity of quartz crystals is something like 18 times stronger at the tip than through the sides. This is why Amethyst druse pieces are used to cleanse other crystals.

In contrast to the warming of crystals in one's hands and other charging methods, the use of Rock Crystal is a completely neutral procedure, during which the effectiveness of the other healing crystals is retained as it is.

For the charging of crystals with Rock Crystal, the healing crystals are either laid on a bed of small tumbled Rock Crystal pieces, or directly on a Rock Crystal group. Both work well, with the Rock Crystal group being clearly the more powerful. As the crystals placed on the Rock Crystal are laid directly on the tips of the crystals, they are charged much more powerfully than when on randomly scattered, tumbled crystal pieces. Either way, the crystals laid on top derive energy, which they absorb and then release again along with their own information. Thus, charging with Rock Crystal groups is a gentle but very effective and, above all, a neutral method.

The most important points about charging on Rock Crystal:
- **Application:** After finishing the cleansing process.
- **Duration:** As desired – unlimited.
- **Suitable for:** All crystals.
- **Please note:** The Rock Crystal groups used for charging have to be cleansed first themselves!

Final Tip

As Amethyst is a quartz-based crystal, it has the ability to charge other crystals as well as to cleanse them. This means that it is not necessary to use additional charging methods if you cleanse with Amethyst, but you can if you want to!

Other Types of Care

Attentiveness and Admiration

Some of the information that crystals absorb (and also transmit again naturally) will be that which we ourselves transmit during our handling of the crystals. Carelessness, thoughtlessness and disrespect are forms of 'information' just as are attentiveness, care, and respect. These kinds of information change the expression of the crystals: if they are treated without attentiveness, they become dull and unattractive; if crystals are handled attentively or even with admiration, they appear virtually to 'blossom'. When I still had my own mineral trade business in the early 1990s, we occasionally had a good look at crystals that had been on sale for a long time, and then deliberately admired them attentively. Lo and behold, just a few days later, they would be sold...

Attentiveness and admiration are among the most appropriate methods of care for our healing crystals or collections of minerals. Far beyond simple (and usually tedious) dusting, or all the other cleansing methods, the above two factors alone bring about the possibility for us to keep our crystals 'fresh'. Simply try this out for yourself!

Changes Within Crystals

Sometimes human influences may even become visible as real changes within a crystal: Rose Quartz and Amethyst may become paler, or even become darker again. The 'snowflakes' (Feldspar crystallizations) within Obsidian may grow, until many a Snowflake Obsidian crystal has become totally grey. Clouding may appear in crystals; or the reverse, crystals become clear again. The list of such changes is long and often very curious...

Obsidian: growth of 'snowflakes' through Feldspar crystallization.

Amethyst: making the violet colour darker is usually only achievable through the effects of radiation.

Many changes within crystals would tend to occur over time: changes in coloration through the influence of light or loss of water, clouding and clearing through changes in tension in the crystal lattice structure, or the 'greying' of some types of Obsidian through gradual crystallization. However, the human factor can at times considerably accelerate such processes! What would normally take years or decades may happen suddenly within weeks or even days.

Regular cleansing on a subtle level may sometimes stop such changes, if they are undesirable, and may even occasionally reverse them – especially with changes in colour or clouding in crystals. However, even if changes can no longer be reversed, this does not mean that the crystal in question has become useless. It has changed – but it may still be a valuable healing crystal!

Water Within Crystals

An important factor for changes occurring in crystals may be the water content of the crystal. If Chrysoprase loses its colour, or the sparkling specks of colour in an Opal begin to disappear, it is usually due to loss of water. The apple green colouring of Chrysoprase only occurs if the nickel contained in the crystal is in contact with water. And the tiny silicic acid beads inside Opal, which break the light, melt into quartz fibres if the crystal dries out. Then Opal turns into Chalcedony – another healing crystal, but not necessarily with the same monetary value.

Chrysoprase: partial bleaching through drying out.

Noble Opal: loss of the rainbow colouring through drying out.

Crystals that contain water should thus be regularly subjected to attentive checking for changes. If they show any signs of water loss, it is recommended to lay the crystals in pH neutral water (with a low calcium content) or, in the case of Opal jewellery, to pack it in moist cotton wool.

This helps regenerate the water content, which may also save the Opal's appearance if such measures are taken in time.

> Loss of water may be the root of loss of colour or other changes in the following crystals: Andes Opal, Noble Opal, Fire Opal, ordinary colourful Opal, pink Chalcedony, green Chalcedony, Chrysoprase, Water Agate. Thus, these crystals should never be laid directly in a bed of salt for cleansing purposes, as salt has a hygroscopic (water-absorbing) effect!

Storage

When considering where to store or keep your crystals, apart from the usual care that has to be taken such as dusting (dust-free glass cases are highly recommended for the purpose!) and regular cleansing and washing, another important point to consider is that healing crystals that are stored close to each other are quite capable of 'informing' each other. A colleague in my former company once experienced this in a very impressive manner when she wanted to carry out exercises with Rock Crystal and Fire Opal in a workshop situation. Since both crystals had been transported in her handbag, the Rock Crystal had suddenly developed Fire Opal characteristics!

Neutral crystals, Rock Crystal in particular, will rapidly absorb information from other healing crystals. In principle, however, all crystals may absorb information from other crystals and will thus also change their influence!

Keeping one's healing crystals like sweets in a large bowl is therefore not really a good idea, unless you intend thorough cleansing of all the crystals before applying them for anything at all. One or two centimetres distance between the crystals, in a glass case for example, will considerably reduce that mutual 'informing' action. Even better, storing the crystals in a display box made of wood that has small wooden compartments has a wonderfully shielding effect.

For the rest, when storing, one should be aware that crystals not only unfold a certain influence when worn with direct body contact, but also when being kept in one's immediate surroundings. A chaotic muddle, or collections arranged without thought or sensitivity, will have a commensurate effect! Clear order is generally much more pleasant all round.

By storing crystals in such a way that we perceive their appearance as aesthetically pleasing, we also actually create beneficial harmony in our surroundings. A sense of aesthetics is nothing other than a refined sense of harmony!

Protection and Purification

The Flow of Information Within a Human Being

Among humans, as with crystals, exchange of information on all levels plays a vital role. Our complex system of spirit, soul, intellect and body can only be coordinated and steered by means of multiple flows of information. Thus, in our bodies alone we possess a whole range of data-highways (nerves, blood vessels, meridians), and 'radio contacts' (light impulses from cell nucleus to cell nucleus). With regard to the soul, the mind, and the spirit, there are additional energetic and telepathic connections.

Without entering into a discussion about the details of this complex system,* one can already get an inkling that undisrupted functioning of all those levels will only be possible if the right kinds of information are exchanged without hindrance and are circulated in the best way possible. The wrong kind of information, at the wrong time, in the wrong place, will inevitably lead to disruptions, although our 'system of communication' is still able to balance most of these disturbances through connecting in parallel and with counter control processes. Only if a certain disruption becomes 'permanent', so to speak, and thus leads to mistakes and possibly further disturbances as a consequence, will we gradually perceive this as feeling uncomfortable, as detrimental effects, as misperceptions or finally, in the form of psychological and physical complaints.

Seen in this way, diseases are simply disruptions in the flow of information caused by persistent 'false information'. The best example for this is allergies. If a certain substance creates the 'last straw situation' in an organism already overloaded through food sensitivity, early illnesses, residues of medications, environmental toxins, stress, and much more, the body may store the information of that last trigger as being connected to all the unpleasant consequences. Such a substance, or even its information alone (!) will then, in future, be sufficient to cause a violent protective reaction – thus an allergy is born!

Dissolving Disturbances

When applying healing crystals to a person, we are essentially trying to cause the regulatory systems to pay attention to the existing disturbance through a similar piece of information ('like heals like'), or, we are transmitting a resolving concept for the disturbance by means of a different piece of information. A crystal that demonstrates a healing effect, therefore, is either providing a similar kind of information, or, possesses different, dissolving-cleansing information.

Certain healing crystals are therefore something like 'general cleaners'. They trigger test processes in our internal communications systems, and self-repairing of disturbances. In this way, they can be employed for 'cleansing processes' in an unspecified manner as they support one's own self-cleansing and self-healing processes.

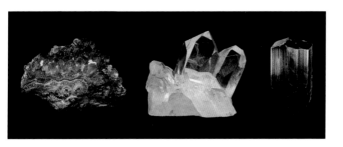

Protection Through Healing Crystals

Naturally (wouldn't you know it!), Amethyst, with its message, 'Liberate yourself of all attachments!' is one of those 'general cleaner' crystals. Also, of course, Rock Crystal, with its information, 'Be who you are!' The third one in this cleansing and protecting alliance is Schorl, or Black Tourmaline. Its message in this context can be defined as 'Let go of anything that does not belong to you!'

Each individual one of these crystals can be applied in many ways for the dissolving and purifying of persistent 'foreign information'. If we stroke the energy field around our bodies (the 'aura') with pieces of Amethyst druse, for example, from top to bottom, we set just such a general cleansing process in motion, which manifests immediately and perceptibly as the dissolving of tensions or the lowering of blood pressure.* It is sufficient, for example, to use an Amethyst comb. On a spiritual level, we then perceive the dissolving

and liberation through Amethyst as the arrival of inner peace.

Rock Crystal brings about a rather gentler clearing process, if it is drunk regularly as gem water. The constant reminder, 'Be who you are!'

makes us more awake and conscious regarding all foreign and/or disruptive influences. We therefore automatically correct disruptive elements and prevent, by and for ourselves, the settling of false information. The result is then perceived in the form of clarity and being 'at peace with oneself'.

With Schorl (Black Tourmaline) it is sufficient simply to wear it on one's body as a necklace, a pendant or a bracelet, to set in motion dissolving and cleansing processes. Schorl is the

* Michael Gienger, The Healing Crystal First Aid Manual, Findhorn/Earthdancer, 2004.

'blockage remover' par excellence and will even attack larger disruptions, which we are holding onto because of guilt, a bad conscience, or simply through stubborn ignoring. By addressing these blockages through Schorl's information, 'Let go that which does not belong to you!', some spiritual matters also naturally begin to shift. This is mirrored in the physical body through increased bowel activity right through to diarrhoea – yet another cleansing process! However, Schorl not only churns one up, but also quickly helps one to let go. We experience this effect of Schorl very clearly as a feeling of relief or indirectly as rapid recovery, better sleep, deep relaxation and greater resistance to stress.

The combination of Amethyst, Rock Crystal and Schorl (Black Tourmaline) is a wonderful cleansing and protecting mixture for many situations in life. Prepared as a gem water, it will suffice to spray the mixture around the body with a pump action spray bottle, within the energy field surrounding the body – the aura. This energy field has a direct connection with our communications system, which is why such applications work very quickly and very directly.

In situations where we can clearly sense that more and more foreign information is attaching itself to us, this mixture as a gem water spray will have an immediately relieving and liberating effect! It had its 'baptism of fire' at the minerals conference in Munich in 2005. Maybe you are familiar with that sensation of gradually becoming more and more 'sticky' and laden with attachments when you are present in a large room full of many people and minerals. You feel tense, as if you have dragged around tons

of weight; there is pressure in your head; a feeling of tiredness (exhaustion); increasing unwillingness and thoughts of escaping – all of these are possibly expressions of the fact that we are full, right up to our eyeballs, with energies and information that we have absorbed. The protective mixture of Amethyst, Rock Crystal and Schorl (Black Tourmaline) as a gem water spray, used once, or, in an emergency, sprayed around one's self several times every few minutes, will rapidly lead to a feeling of relief and liberation. When the mixture was still in its 'test phase' in 2005, it proved itself on at least forty occasions at the minerals conference. Unfortunately, then the bottle was empty...

We can mentally support this self-purification process, and the protection derived from it, through a thought message addressed to all attached energies and information; '*Return to your origin, or be liberated!*'

This mental liberation process can be used any time we have no healing crystals to hand...

Attachments in Rooms

Foreign energies and information can not only become attached to crystals and other objects, or to the communications systems of other living beings, but can also become anchored in rooms or certain other places. This happens partly through events that have occurred at that place; partly through thoughts, which were directed at that place against people and events at those places; or simply through the 'ballast' others off-loaded and left at that place. I often come across the latter at places where seminars have been held. This phenomenon has been known from time immemorial, which is why all cultures all over the world have developed cleansing, purifying and clearing measures for rooms and places.

In principle, these are the same methods that are described in this booklet for the cleansing of crystals.

Clearing Rooms

Burning incense and cleansing through sound are the first port of call in many cultures for the purification and clearing of rooms, with the latter preferably being loud and dissonant. A very vivid impression of this, for example, is the musical introductions to Tibetan ceremonies. Even the most stubborn demon will not withstand such methods! The noise and cacophony at carnival time in some European countries, and the racket created by fireworks at New Year, even the loud ringing of church bells are all derived from the same idea and purpose. Bells rung before a storm were originally not just meant as a warning, but were intended to discharge the electrically-charged atmosphere before a thunderstorm by means of sound waves.

Corresponding to the intensity of sounds, many cultures also use the burning of incense on a massive scale. Not only are shamanic ceremonies often pregnant with dense smoke, even the incense burner in Catholic churches is often filled up well and swung about vigorously.

We too can use singing bowls and incense sticks on a smaller scale for the cleansing of rooms. The important thing is that every corner and nook

and cranny of the room is smoked and filled with sound. After a short while of allowing this to 'work in', the room should be vigorously aired.

Salt Crystal Lamps

Salt, as already mentioned above, is very popular for the cleansing of rooms; it used to be sprinkled in rooms and cattle sheds, or thrown in front of the wedding procession, and always served for the cleansing of rooms and the atmosphere, and for the cleansing of the moods of all participants at births, baptisms, during meals or sleep, during the fasting period, when beginning a journey, on the death bed, or at a burial.

This ancient tradition is enjoying continuity in our modern times in the form of salt lamps. Because of the purifying and protective qualities of salt, these lamps play their part in the purification and clearing of rooms.*

In addition to the sheer aesthetics of its beautiful gentle light, there is the information of the salt itself: 'Cleanse and purify yourself!', which causes the positive effects of these lamps.

Cleansing and Protective Mixture

For the cleansing and the clearing of rooms, a gem water mixture of Amethyst, Diamond, Fluorite, Topaz and Black Tourmaline (Schorl) has proved itself effective. In it is the combination the following information, and a high degree of purifying power:

Amethyst: 'Liberate yourself from all attachments!'
Diamond: 'Invincible freedom!'
Fluorite: 'It's alright now!'
Schorl: 'Let go that which does not belong here!'
Topaz: 'Preserve your own space!'

Amethyst, Diamond and Schorl ensure deep-reaching purification; Fluorite returns the natural order of things, and Topaz helps to protect the liberated space thus derived.

This mixture is very powerful and so intense that it is recommended to leave the room immediately after spraying the gem water mixture and to air the room thoroughly fifteen to thirty minutes later. If you remain in the room, this mixture may activate very intense physical cleansing processes (diarrhoea, profuse sweating, etc.), which is often not at all desirable.

It goes without saying that you can support the cleansing of a room mentally through the thought message addressed to all attached energies and information, 'Return to your origin, or be free!'

Self-regulating Systems

Healing crystals may also provide a further important cleansing and protective function in rooms. They are not only helpful during an active clearing process, they may also build up a self-regulating cleansing and protective system if they are set up in the form of larger crystals, groups of crystals and druses in a room.

Again, it is Amethyst ('Liberate yourself from all attachments!'), Rock Crystal ('Be yourself!'), and Black Tourmaline (Schorl) ('Let go of all that does not belong here!') that have proven beneficial for the creation of self-regulating and protective systems. Amethyst is used here in the shape of a druse, and Rock Crystal and Schorl are in the form of freestanding individual crystals.

If you wish to set up a system of this type, it is very important that you first check, through a quiet meditation or silent devotion, whether the room in question actually requires such a cleansing and protective system. Sit down quietly in the room, or dwell there in your thoughts, and pose the following question to the room: 'Will it be beneficial for all beings to set up a cleansing and protective system with healing crystals in this room?' It should be clear in your intention that your concern is the wellbeing of all participating beings, even if one or the other of the affected beings is not at that moment particularly enthusiastic about the idea (otherwise you will just get the result of an opinion poll...). The question is asked in order to find out whether the process would be beneficial from a higher point of view.

If your intention is clear you will receive a clear answer, which may manifest as a thought, a feeling, a sensation, a physical manifestation, or even as a seemingly 'coincidental' external phenomenon. However it comes, you will perceive whether this answer will motivate you to carry on or whether you get the impression it would be better to scrap the intention. If the answer turns out to be affirmative, you may then set up the crystals in the room: one Amethyst druse, one Rock Crystal group and a free-standing Schorl crystal.

Possibly the three crystals will appear in your mind's eye in particular sizes and/or arrangements in the room, and you will immediately get a coherent impression. Memorize the sizes and the arrangement, or immediately make a sketch. Otherwise, simply vary the sizes and the arrangement of the crystals in your mind until a coherent impression arises. Not having to actually move the crystals around allows you to freely play and order things until they feel right. When the impression coincides with what feels right to you, remember the sizes and the arrangement and immediately make the sketch.

This initial exercise is helpful for finding the right crystals and setting them up in the right way. It provides you with an idea of that which you are seeking and how the crystals should be arranged. There are no generally applicable rules, as every room is unique.

It is also very important for you to understand that this exercise is an 'approximate orientation' and that you do not have to slavishly adhere to your vision of how it should be done. In the end, the impression of the actual crystals will decide which ones you choose (and your purse may certainly play a part in all this). And, last of all, it is your impression of the room after setting up the crystals that will decide whether they are properly placed. If you need to, change things around until everything feels right! And remember, the facts of the room should be taken into

consideration. A crystal that is always in the way will be more irritating than useful. In the end, it is only you that has to approve it.

Close the setting up procedure with a little ceremony of your own. You have now constructed a self-regulating cleansing and protective system with three crystals, through which foreign energies and information will themselves find their way back to their origins, or become liberated.

As part of your ceremony, you may also add to each individual one of the crystals a thought message for their cleansing and protective functions. The following simple sentence encompasses the entire essence of protection and purification:

Return to your origin, or be free!

Appendix

The Author

Michael Gienger has been collecting minerals since 1972 and, from 1985 onwards, has immersed himself in the subjects of crystal healing and the energetic qualities of crystals. Michael has also gained international acclaim through his research into crystal healing. He is the author of more than twenty publications, a number of which have become standard works in their field and have been translated into eleven languages so far. In addition to his activities as an author and publisher of the Cairn Elen editions of Neue Erde, Michael Gienger also gives lectures and seminars on crystal healing and related topics.

For further information, see: www.michael-gienger.de, www.steinheilkunde.de, www.fairtrademinerals.de, www.edelstein-massagen.de, www.cairn-elen.de

Thanks

For the impulse that resulted in this little book, many thanks to Sabine Schneider-Kuehnle and Marco Schreier; also for all their support with ideas, inspirations, and materials! Thanks also goes to Ines Blersch for the beautiful photographs; to Anja Birkholz for her enthusiastic commitment as the photographic model; to Peter Walter for his assistance in the studio; to Fred Hageneder of Dragon Design for his excellent design and layout; and to Andreas Lentz, my publisher, for his kindly support and the fast realization of the project. Very special thanks goes to Erwin Engelhardt, Wolfgang Die, Walter von Holst, Monika Grundmann and Joachim Goebel for much inspiration on the subject, as well as to all the people who, over the last twenty years, have reported their experiences with the different methods. Only with their help was it possible to create this little volume.

Heartfelt thanks!